SIMPLY ORGANIZED

KITCHENS

SIMPLY ORGANIZED KITCHENS

Creating an organized kitchen to bring families back to the dinner table

By

Melissa Schmalenberger, J.D.

Dedicated to my parents, Allan and Georgiann,
the world's greatest organizers;

my husband Ray, who maintains my systems with a smile on his
face and love in his heart;

my children—Tyler, Jackson, and Carter—for their love, support,
and the lessons in perseverance they taught me.

I am forever grateful. I love you all.

Table of Contents

Introduction

As a professional organizer, I often hear two complaints:

- 🌀 *"My kitchen is so small, I just don't have enough room."*
- 🌀 *"I have too much stuff in my kitchen and I can't find anything."*

There is good news for both of these common problems. Have you heard of the Pareto Principle or the 80-20 rule? In essence you use 20% of your stuff 80% of the time. This book will help you figure out which 20% of the stuff you use in your kitchen so you can shed the leftovers.

Gone are the days of expensive and lengthy kitchen remodels. Over the years, I've saved clients thousands of dollars by organizing their kitchens. We repurpose drawers and cabinets, finding new space where they thought none existed.

Would you like to reclaim your kitchen and make smart use of your space?

Now is the time to give up items in your kitchen that you never use. I once had a ceramic mold to make gingerbread houses. In twelve years, I never once made a gingerbread house. We all hold onto sentimental items way too long, hoping to make wonderful memories in the kitchen with our children. In reality, we just want to get dinner on the table.

I intentionally created this book to be short and accessible. My goal is for you to actually complete the steps. I don't want you to be stuck reading a book for hours. I want you sitting on your kitchen floor mining for the most important items. This book should not collect dust. It is an action book to help produce an organized kitchen that functions for you and your family.

Before you start, grab a box or two (or more) for items you plan to donate. Make sure boxes aren't too large; they get heavy by the time you are done. During the process, document what you shed. Count the bags and boxes that leave your house. Take before and after pictures. It is nice to look back and see how hard you worked!

Most of my clients are concerned that they simply don't have the time it takes to get their kitchen organized. Not everyone has a professional organizer nearby to do the task, nor the budget to make the magic happen. But I'm here to say that if you can follow the steps in this convenient manual, you will have a clean and organized kitchen in less than thirty days. Schedule a reasonable daily time commitment, usually fifteen to sixty minutes. Some days will require more, some less. The good news? Once you complete this initial overhaul, you will spend less time staying organized in upcoming years. So set aside some time and let's get organized!

What to do with items you no longer need? Ask around your community, at your place of worship, the local soup kitchen, or an area women's shelter. There are always places looking for gently used donations.

As you organize the inside of each cabinet and drawer, take the time to scrub it with hot, soapy water.

I suggest you read this book through from beginning to end a few times. If you read a tip from Day 20 that might be more profitable for your kitchen on Day 11, make a note on those pages. Every kitchen is different. Every person is different. Use this twenty-one-day guide to inspire you and to keep you on track.

Some ideas may not work for you; you might think of things I have not covered. I simply hope you learn some organizing skills along the way to help you troubleshoot on your own and solve your specific problems. Use the handy checklist, located at the back of the book, to track your success.

Now that you've prepared to transform your kitchen into a place of culinary magnificence, let's start. On your mark, get set ... GO!

Day 1

Cabinet fronts

A clean kitchen is the sign of a wasted life.

~ Anonymous

Plan on putting in more time this first day than on the ones following. Don't worry; take a deep breath and get it done. Find a partner to help. For me, it was my husband who would pull down dusty décor that I quickly washed and dried.

Could your wooden cabinets use some wood conditioner? Orange oil? Elbow grease? What about the baseboards? I even took time to clean the dingy spots where the baseboard meets the floor.

This is a good day to evaluate your cabinet hardware. Does it need to be cleaned? Beware abrasive cleansers; they can cause corrosion over time. Are hinges, handles, or knobs loose? Now is a good time to tighten them with a screwdriver.

Are you ready for a change? Tired of shiny brass, I bought a can of oil-rubbed, bronze spray paint. That little afternoon project updated my kitchen for the cost of sweat equity and a single can of paint. (A few years later, I updated with new hardware—expensive, but a huge "wow" factor.)

Hot Tips

- Do you have upper open shelving? Open shelves attract a layer of greasy dust. After you scrub them, cover the area with newspaper. (It will never be seen from below.) Next time you clean, simply reline with fresh newspapers. You will never have to scrub that gunk again!
- Use an old toothbrush to scrub deep grooves and hard-to-reach nooks and crannies.
- If you prefer an organic degreaser, fill a spray bottle with equal amounts of distilled white vinegar and water. A cabinet that is especially greasy may need to be sprayed a time or two.

We moved fourteen months ago, and I am amazed at the dirt and dust in crevices, even with regular cleaning! No wonder people did spring cleaning. Too many dust bunnies took up residence over the winter. This is a real reminder that once-a-year deep cleaning is good practice!

~ Dawn

Day 2

Utensils and tools

A kitchen without a knife is not a kitchen.

~ Masaharu Morimoto

Gather all utensils in one place to begin the sorting process. Include knives and anything hiding in the dishwasher.

Discard or recycle anything broken or damaged. Food particles and bacteria might be lurking in a cracked wooden spoon.

Next, group like items and take a hard look at the duplicates. Do you have fifteen silicone spatulas but only use three? Get rid of twelve and keep the ones you always grab first. Do you have three sets of measuring cups? Keep one and donate the others. I replaced mine with one beautiful set. If I do a lot of baking in one day, I quickly wash, dry, and keep going, never missing the extras I once owned. Ditto for my knives.

Organize all the "keepers" with drawer dividers (but only after you've wiped the inside of each drawer).

My handiest cooking utensils—wooden spoons, tongs, ladle—are at my fingertips in an attractive container next to the stove.

Examine your knives. Are they sharp? If not, sharpen them yourself or take them to a professional. Store them near the area where you chop and slice food.

Not sure what you really use? Caught up in the I-might-need-it-someday syndrome? Place questionable items in a box labeled with a date six to twelve months in the future. As you need an item, remove it from the box. At the cut-off date, donate the entire box without opening and inspecting the contents. Now you will know exactly what you use!

Hot Tips

- If you have plenty of counter space, think about placing your most-used tools in a caddy. To avoid the large one-size-fits-everything crock, select only a few utensils and use a smaller pitcher or jar.
- Start with an empty countertop caddy and, as you cook throughout the week, fill it with the tools that you go back to time and again. Once you've reached six, stop and reanalyze. If your kitchen counters are crowded, skip this step.
- If a knife block consumes precious counter space, consider storing knives in a drawer or on a magnetic wall strip.

For some time, I've had a couple of storage containers full of surplus utensils to see if I use any of them. Last night, I commented about all the potholders we have in our potholder drawer. My husband rolled his eyes and said, "Why don't you put them in the Tupperware container with everything else and see if you ever use them!"

~ Patti

Day 3

Plasticware

I only have a kitchen because it came with the house.

~ Anonymous

Do you have enough plastic storage containers and water bottles to stock a dollar store? It's time to purge!

Your first step is to match lids with containers and recycle any orphans. While you're at it, dispose of containers never intended for long-term food storage—like yogurt and sour cream tubs. Many of these are made with chemicals that are harmful when heated in a microwave oven.

Which containers have not been used in the last six months? Do you have a deviled egg holder taking up precious space? An unwieldy pie transporter? Think about donating them.

Try nesting the remaining plastic containers to take up as little room as possible.

Store lids in a drawer, or beneath the nested containers, or under the sink in a magazine holder.

Remember to wipe the storage areas.

Hot Tips

- If you have an overabundance of fast food cups or souvenir mugs, remove and recycle them. Because it's difficult to know which are safe to use, I've converted to stainless steel and glass for drinking. When I "win" yet another plastic water bottle, it goes straight to my donation box.
- Consider replacing plasticware with glass containers, especially for food that will be microwaved. Margarine tubs are not food storage containers. Be safe and be smart.

I fished out plastic lids and cups hiding in deep corners. I reclaimed two-thirds of the lazy Susan cabinet by recycling plasticware and donating the egg cooker I've held onto since high school graduation forty years ago. Feeling good!

~ Susan

Day 4

Specialty appliances and serving dishes

In department stores, so much kitchen equipment is bought indiscriminately by people who just come in for men's underwear.

~ Julia Child

Specialty appliances refer to items such as fondue pots, food processors, pressure cookers, juicers, mixers, dehydrators, snow cone machines, toaster ovens, gelato makers, egg cookers ... I see it all. Serving dishes include oddities like gravy boats, egg cups, candy dishes, tiered cake stands, escargot plates (yes, there really is such a thing), and punchbowls.

Which large kitchen appliances and servers do you rarely use? Do you only pull out your waffle maker and turkey roaster twice each year? Do you have a food processor or serving platter that is taking up cupboard space? Have you used them in the last six months? Do you see yourself using them in the next six months?

Could they be stored in another area of the home? Would it make sense to store them in a closet, basement, garage, attic? Otherwise, donate.

Hot Tips

- If you rarely use an appliance or dish but *must* store it in the kitchen, consider using a hard-to-access area like top shelves or behind other dishes. Save your prime real estate—what you can reach without bending or needing a stepstool—for those appliances you access most often. Like your toaster or smoothie maker.

- Can your item do double duty? I now have an Instant Pot (pressure cooker) that has replaced my slow cooker and my rice cooker. Instead of merely adding a third appliance to my kitchen I was able to dispose of two. I have a neutral white serving platter that I use to serve the turkey once a year. I repurpose it to serve appetizers or large salads when I entertain.

- If you live in a place where your cooking styles vary with the season, plan your kitchen's prime real estate to do the same. During grilling season, my grilling supplies come forward and my slow cooker goes to the back. If you fire up the blender in the summer, place it where it's easily accessible.

Upper-story, I-need-a-ladder cabinets are typical storage for seasonal or holiday ware. (Why do designers even create them?) If you don't use what's up there, donate the items *now*.

This kitchen challenge has made me rethink what to keep, challenged me to find new uses for things I want to keep or can't part with, and encouraged me to get rid of things I forgot I had.

~ Candy

Day 5

Pots and pans

In the childhood memories of every good cook, there's a large kitchen, a warm stove, a simmering pot, and a mom.

~ Barbara Costikyan

When my clients need more room, I look first at their pots and pans. Often cabinets are jammed. Pots without lids. Lids without pots. Pans never used. This is an area where almost everyone can pare down.

I usually find we can eliminate nearly half and gain much needed space in the very heart of our homes—our kitchens.

Pile all pots, pans, and lids in one spot so that you can assess what you have. And wipe out those cabinets while they're empty! Pair lids with the pots and pans. Did you find a lid with no match? Sometimes I get rid of the pan but forget about the lid. You, too?

Evaluate what you have. Do you use it? Can some items do double duty? Do you need every saucepan or only the two you use? Do you need four sizes of frying pans?

I know it's difficult to break up matching sets, but I give you permission. However, if a complete set is more important than the space they inhabit ... well, it's your choice.

Assess your storage area. Place pots and pans you most often use to the front of the cabinet. Placing heavy skillets on a low shelf, although often necessary, can strain your back. Because I cook in it several times weekly and it is attractive, I keep my heavy Dutch oven sitting on my range.

Nesting pots and pans with or without their lids is a guessing game. Do they stack well? Will the nonstick coating get scratched? If you rarely use lids, store them somewhere else, such as the drawer under the stove. If you have space for it, a dish drying rack conveniently organizes them. Slide it to the back of the cabinet if the lids are rarely used.

Hot Tips

- Not all kitchens are equipped with back-saving rollout shelves. My husband retrofitted ours with a kit that cost less than $100 and took about fifteen minutes to install. Is this an option for you?
- Not certain which pots, pans, and lids you use? Place a brightly colored sticky note on each and label it with today's

date. When you use the item, remove the note. At the end of six months, dispose of anything still wearing a sticky note. Warning: This practice should be limited to possessions in your life, not the people in your life. Then, again ...

I found two lids that had no pots to match. Weird. I threw away anything with a ding or chip, sick of keeping crap like that.
Why do I do that?

~ Beth

Day 6

Cookbooks and recipes

Most of my recipes start life in the domestic kitchen, and even those that start
out in the restaurant kitchen have to go through
the domestic kitchen.

~ Yotam Ottolenghi

D o you have recipes and cookbooks all over your kitchen and home? Gather them in one place. (Are you sensing a theme throughout the organizational process?)

Take a serious look at your cookbooks and keep only those you actually use or think you will use in the near future. Send the others off to a new home like a library or bookstore or your sister-in-law's kitchen. If a cookbook has only a few recipes you use, take the time now to copy them so you can donate the book.

Create folders (or binders) for recipes you clip from magazines and newspapers. Sort them into categories: Appetizers, Breakfast, Soups, Salads, Breads, Beef, Pork, Chicken, Fish, Pasta/Rice, Vegetables, Sweets, and Take Out menus. Keep only those you truly plan to try. Store them in a vertical file holder in a kitchen cabinet.

Hot Tips

- Consider going digital. There are great online sources to help store and organize your recipes. I use Microsoft OneNote. I can type in a word from the recipe, do a search, and *voilà!* it appears. Or, use your scanner and go completely paperless once and for all. Of course, I preserve any sentimental recipes handwritten by my grandma.

- Use Pinterest as a go-to resource. I have a board called "Food I Have Made" where I search for my successful recipes. I categorize my boards much like those I listed above.

- Use an app on your phone. I take photos of recipes and save them (on my phone) in a folder I titled "Recipes." This makes them easy to search and I can zoom in to read the ingredients.

I put loose recipe clippings on a recipe card and filed in the recipe box. Focusing only on cookbooks and recipes was key. I caught myself trying to repair a broken necklace, and quickly put it aside.

~ Susan

Day 7

Family favorite recipes

I do my part to keep the planet green—just look in my refrigerator.

~ Annonymous

Most families tend to fix the same meals again and again. My now adult sons will joke that we only made three dishes in our household: homemade mac and cheese, chicken chipotle tacos, and chicken curry. In defense, I claim that I'm really a great cook and love to make a variety of foods.

But, let's face it. When you have several people you're trying to please and one despises ground meat, one refuses to eat vegetables, and one only likes white, colorless food … Picky eaters make it difficult for the cook to be creative!

Consequently, I fell into a routine that revolved around the same few recipes.

Save yourself some time by gathering *your* family's favorite recipes in one spot, in one system.

Make a list of your family's favorite twenty-one meals (if you can scrape together that many). Take the time to write them on recipe cards or type them into your computer or smartphone. Organize and save the recipes conveniently so that you can pull up the recipes on your phone while you are grocery shopping. You will always know exactly what to buy.

Hot Tips:

- Find your favorite side dishes and desserts at the same time. When you have all of these in one place, it is really easy to figure out what to make for dinner on a daily, weekly, or even monthly basis. You no longer will hear the question, "What's for dinner?"
- There is an app for that! There are so many choices for apps to manage your recipes and grocery lists ... too many to list. Apps are always being updated and new ones are always on the horizon. Search your app store and read the reviews. Download a few and see what works for you!

I bought a small ScanSnap scanner, like NeatReceipts but cheaper and online at Costco. Now receipts that land with all the paper mess—and even the kids' schedules—can be run through the scanner and sent to my phone. I'm not always faithful, but I love it when I am!

~ Jean

Day 8

Glasses and cups

It's so hard when I have to ... and so easy when I want to.

~ Annie Gottlieb

You already know the routine: Gather all the glasses and cups from every nook and cranny in your house—even the ones in the bathrooms and on the nightstands. And under the teenager's bed. And, yes, wipe the cabinet shelves.

Reduce by throwing away any that are cracked or chipped. You could easily cut a lip on imperfect glass. Besides, bacteria can live in those cracks.

Sort into groups: coffee cups, drinking glasses, sports bottles, stemware, mugs. Begin to look at these as sets. Do you have a lone juice glass that nobody uses? Do you have coffee mugs but no coffee

19

drinkers? Do you have drinking glasses with your bank's logo? Set aside those you find serviceable and appealing, but donate the remainder.

Now, place the "keepers" in a designated cabinet in organized rows. For example, put coffee cups on the right, juice glasses on the left, drinking glasses in the middle. Take advantage of adjustable shelves to avoid wasting vertical space in your cupboards.

Do you need additional or alternative storage ideas? Wine glasses and mugs or cups can be hung in specialty racks or by hooks created just for this purpose.

Place glasses that are used most often within arm's reach of your family. If you have small children, you may want to place theirs in a lower cabinet.

Hot Tips

- Store frequently used glasses near the dishwasher for ease of unloading.
- Limit everyone in your family to one water glass or coffee cup per day. Too often, the top of my dishwasher was full of glasses, but no longer since we implemented this practice. How much energy and water could we save if we used the same glass all day long? How many glasses could you get rid of if everybody used only one?

I started with glasses and my cupboards are now cleaned and organized. I couldn't believe the variety of things I had held on to, including sippy cups and straws. My kids are teens!

~ Jean

Day 9

Under the sink

Organizing is what you do before you do something, so that when you do it, it is not all mixed up.

~ A. A. Milne

Remember that deep, dark cavern under the sink? It is usually home to things like dish soap, cleansers, rags, pet items, plastic shopping bags, and the kitchen wastebasket. Because of water pipes and garbage disposal, it is an oddly shaped space whose true potential is often overlooked. Here we go again:

Pull out everything—even the bag of dog food—and thoroughly wipe down the floor of the cabinet. Don't forget the sides where garbage might have splattered. Throw away items that are broken or have no immediate use.

Weed out anything that doesn't belong in the kitchen. For example, would it make more sense to store plastic sacks and bags near the dog's leash so they're handy on walks?

Group like items and only keep the amount you really need. I find that people save extra jars to hold the grease from bacon and other meats. How many do you need?

Find containers that will hold the items by group. For example, use a cleaning caddy for cleaning supplies, a small basket for pet items, and a cleaning bucket for rags.

Hot Tips

- This space can get damp so don't store anything under the sink that should never get wet.
- Take advantage of excess vertical space. Look at the sides of cabinets and the insides of their doors where racks or hooks might be mounted.
- Purchase rollout racks to store items.

Although not on the daily task list, I've found extra energy to tackle even more projects—such as emptying and cleaning the household toolbox, which is stored under the kitchen sink.

~ Susan

Day 10

Dishtowels, potholders, and trivets

I liked the energy of cooking, the action, the camaraderie. I often compare the kitchen to sports and compare the chef to a coach. There are a lot of similarities to it.

~ Todd English

If you are like everyone else, you have more dishtowels, dishcloths, and potholders than you know what to do with. When you buy new ones, I bet you don't get rid of the old ones. Why do we do that to ourselves?

Instead, keep only those you use. Designate any extras for rags. If you have too many rags (in good condition), think about giving them to a local veterinarian or animal shelter.

Store dishtowels conveniently near the sink for drying your hands or a dish, or wiping a counter. Likewise, keep potholders and hot pads conveniently near the stove.

Are the drawers overstuffed? You want them to stay tidy and organized each time they close.

Hot Tips

- Designate separate towels for hands. I am a realist and know that when my children wash their hands, they do not wash them super clean. I do not want cross contamination from dirty hands to clean dishes.
- Do you use trivets under hot dishes? Think about using a wooden cutting board to serve this need. One item, two uses.

For some reason I kept towels I hate and that don't dry quickly. By purging, I got rid of more than half. I do laundry often, so have no need for a ton of towels.

~ Beth

Day 11

Information center

I go out to the kitchen to feed the dog,
but that's about as much cooking as I do.

~ Betty White

Kitchens seem to be a magnet for paper clutter. I blame it on the flat surfaces of counters and islands just begging to be heaped. Phone books, sports schedules, school and church directories, family calendars, bills, and invitations all seem to land in the kitchen.

Gather any sheet of paper that can be seen as potential information and start to look at similar themes. Does Johnny have sport schedules that need to be tracked? Does Sammie have a list of Girl Scout badges she's working on? Does Mikey have a monthly snack list you don't want to lose?

Keep only one phone book—the most recent. Don't use phone books anymore? Plop them in the recycle bin. And find an online service that you trust to opt-out of receiving any phone books in the future.

Think about inputting those important but irritating papers into a digital format categorized by family member, topic, or calendar. Once the information is inputted, dispose of the papers.

Hot Tips

- Not ready to go digital? Use the inside of a cabinet door as a message center. When my kids were young, I taped entire lists of phone numbers and school menus inside my cabinet.
- Tape a plastic page protector to the inside of your cabinet to slide in updated papers.
- Paint the inside cabinet doors with chalkboard or magnetic paint. Or cover with a thin layer of corkboard or a sheet of metal. Your new best friends are chalk, magnets, or tacks. (Try hard not to attach papers to the refrigerator, as this merely adds to the cluttered look.)
- If you are computer savvy, consider scanning documents as you get them. Save them to your phone via ScanSnap or NeatReceipts. Or save the documents in OneNote or Evernote.

Created an information center while on hold with Blue Cross Blue Shield! I turned on the speakerphone and used those eighteen minutes to find my label maker and tackle the paper mess. Less stressful than just holding on the line— and something accomplished.

~ Beth

Day 12

Junk drawers

I can direct breakfast, lunch, and dinner. I take pride in my kitchen, but I'm not going to direct a movie.

~ Julia Roberts

L et's face it, every kitchen has one ... or two ... or three ... junk drawers. Now is the time to create a *single, organized* drawer. Choose one that is not too deep, otherwise it will be even harder to locate your rubber bands and thumbtacks.

Dump out the drawer(s) on a flat surface. Vacuum into the corners and wipe clean.

Throw away anything that's broken or has no immediate use.

Weed out things that belong other places and put them in a separate pile. (You'll put those ponytail bands in the bathroom drawer. Later.)

Group like items: pencils in one pile and glue or tape in another.

At this point, you need to assess whether you really need seventeen pens and fifty-four pencils and seven rolls of scotch tape. Remember the 80/20 Rule: Most people use 20% of their items 80% of the time. So before hanging onto something, ask:

- Does it work? If not, toss it.
- When was the last time I used it? If longer than six months, donate it.
- Can I replace it cheaply if I decide to get rid of it?
- Does it take up a lot of room? Perhaps it should be stored somewhere else.
- Have I kept this orphan cell phone charger for three years even though I'll probably never figure out where it really belongs?

Place the "keeper" items back in the drawer. If you don't have a drawer organizer, now is the time to get one. Do not buy organizational products before you organize. Every drawer is different, and no divider is perfect for every drawer or purpose.

Hot Tips

🍄 To find the right organizational product, assess how many piles you've created. Do you have lots of little items that need mini-containers? Do you have over-sized items that won't fit in a standard-sized divider? Also keep in mind how much space each category requires, which items should be more conveniently located, and what the overall dimensions are for the drawer itself.

🍄 For a new twist, focus only on what you use and get rid of the rest. By focusing on the 20% of the stuff I used, it was simple to dispose of the 80% I knew I wasn't using. (I had marbles rattling around for eight years; now I can honestly say I have lost my marbles—because they aren't in the junk drawer anymore!)

My junk drawer took one hour to empty and clean. Then I sorted and tossed unknown items. My husband loved helping out; he found screws, bolts, tools he can use in his farm shop.

~ Susan

Day 13

Plates and bowls

I like hugs and I like kisses, but what I'd love ...

is help with the dishes.

~ Anonymous

You're more than half done culling and reorganizing your kitchen. Let's tackle the next phase.

Gather plates and bowls from every nook and cranny in your house, including the cereal bowl under your daughter's pillow. Discard any that are cracked or chipped. (Remember? Cuts and bacteria!)

Place like items together. Do you have character plates the kids have outgrown? Saucers that belong to the partial set you never use?

Place the remainder in a—freshly washed—cabinet or two. Put those most frequently used within a handy arm's reach of your family.

Factor in height: My shorter clients need to easily reach these daily used items; I am tall, and I like things to be high so I don't have to stoop.

Stack same-sized plates and bowls together. Add wire shelves to maximize cupboard space. It is never fun to lift a stack of plates in order to get to the ones below.

Make certain often-used plates and bowls are conveniently shelved near the dishwasher.

Hot Tips

- Keep plates, platters, serving dishes, and bowls that are used infrequently on the top shelf of a cabinet.
- Have you thought about shelves within shelves? If you have a stack of bowls on top of the plates, think about using a portable shelf that can hold and separate the two sets of items. They take up little room but add much needed functionality.
- If you have young children, put their placemats, plates, cups, and bowls in a lower cabinet. They can unload the dishwasher and put their own items away.

I've been going to the wrong cupboard for glasses and plates since I completed this challenge. Tough to teach an old dog a new trick after seventeen years! I do like the change, however. Hubby has been gone for three weeks and will be home tomorrow. Let the real challenge begin!

~ Patti

Day 14

Spices

A messy kitchen is a sign of a good meal.

~ Anonymous

If you cook a lot, chances are you own more than twenty spices. If you rarely cook, chances are you have salt and pepper and maybe some cinnamon. I fall in the "more" camp, with over seventy at one count, so I must be creative with my storage, just as you may need to be.

Look at expiration dates. If you have spices that are still in metal tins, they are probably more than ten years old and need to go.

Did you buy mace and can't remember why or don't have a recipe that calls for it? Get rid of any spices that you know you are never going to use.

Check for duplicates. Do you have three pumpkin pie spices because you keep buying them at Thanksgiving? Can you consolidate them into one container? Or keep the freshest and discard the rest if you know you are never going to use it by the time it expires.

Store your seasonings away from heat and humidity yet readily accessible for cooking and baking. I use a corner cabinet that holds lazy Susans, one in the back corner and two toward the front, making it easy to read and reach every spice with a simple spin. These turntables may also be purchased with a second tier.

Think about taking the time to alphabetize your spices. It's a one-time chore: As you cook you will return the spice to its empty spot.

Hot Tips

- Store seasonings in a cool, dark place. As tempting as it may be, do not store them near the stove. Heat and humidity are not friendly to your spices, and you will find that they will not stay as fresh.

- I have gone from owning over seventy-five spices to only seventeen. Why did I have cream of tartar when I never use a sugar cookie recipe that called for it? It was easy to detect which spices I use; they were at the front of the cabinet, nearly empty and covered with sticky fingerprints. I curated to what I only need and disposed of the rest. I poured my spices into beautiful glass jars and added labels.

- Combine two half-used spice containers into one.

I appreciate walking into my kitchen and opening cupboards and drawers and seeing less stuff in a more organized location. I love that you have the process broken down. Even when I have gotten behind by a couple of days, I feel like I can do this if I just keep plugging away one day at a time.

~ Darla

Day 15

Food wraps and plastic bags

If you can't stand the heat, get out of the kitchen.

~ Harry Truman

I f you cook, you most likely own slim boxes of aluminum foil, plastic wrap, wax paper, parchment paper, sandwich bags, and plastic food bags of various sizes. Because they aren't a standard size, organizing them is problematic.

Once again, only keep what you know you are going to use. If you bought parchment paper for one recipe that you are never going to make again, now is the time to get rid of it. Do your really use three different sizes of storage bags?

Take the ones that you use seasonally and place them somewhere else in the home. I am referring specifically to that oversized container of aluminum foil!

To bring families back to the dinner table

Look at alternative storage solutions. Shop for wire wrap racks that can be installed on pantry doors or hung from an existing shelf. Do you have space between your refrigerator and your upper kitchen cabinet? Could you slide a slim letter basket with these items in that unused space?

No alternative storage? Find an empty drawer. Place those you use most frequently at a height that doesn't cause you to bend.

Hot Tips

- If you have extra height left in a cabinet, create a second shelf about four to five inches tall to store all your boxes of wraps at eye level. This takes up little space and can free up a drawer.
- Can you store wraps and bags in a drawer with other items? I now have mine sitting on top of my cutting boards. They are easy to grab, and it made sense to combine the two drawers into one.

The process made me think of what I really need in my kitchen. I'm learning you don't have to do it all at once. It's okay to do a little at a time and it will eventually get finished!

~ Stacey

39

Day 16

Kitchen counters

Cleanliness is very important. If you let kids make a total mess in the kitchen and then leave, you're not really teaching them anything.

~ Emeril Lagasse

Kitchen counters are usually the place where everything lands that does not have a home. We eliminated some of the clutter—papers, excess appliances, extra dishware—earlier, but today we focus on the countertops themselves. This is the area people struggle with most.

Counters are where mail, notes from teachers, bills, the toaster, the mixer, napkins, a fruit bowl, canisters, receipts, and maybe even some plants or seasonal decor reside. If you knew what to do with the clutter, it would already be gone. Your goal? To winnow down to the items you use every day or weekly at the very least.

Your countertops are the place to make and prepare a meal. Every family's countertops will look different. We are not a family of coffee drinkers so you will not find a coffeemaker in my kitchen.

This will probably be your longest workday. If you drink wine, pour yourself a glass to sip as you organize. Make sure you are free of distractions, so you can better focus. Then:

- Sweep it all into one space and see what you have.
- Pull out anything outdated, broken—or that belongs elsewhere in the house.
- Separate items you rarely use and find a new home for them. If you only make toast once a month, the toaster should not be on the counter. If you have a spice rack, could you put it in a cabinet? Do you have a utensil caddy, but plenty of drawer space to store them instead?
- Now gather all like items. What do they in common? Do you have a pile of things for each child or spouse? Do you have mail that needs to be opened, bills that need to be paid? Do you have something waiting to be repaired?
- Create a system for processing papers. What about a basket that sits on the counter to hold all loose papers? (Remember to sort and organize it weekly.) I have an upright file box on my kitchen counter when needed, or in a closet when it is not in use. I created files for each category of paper I have. Your categories could include bills to pay, recipes to try, kid's papers to save, pictures to save, etc. When my mail arrives, it goes into one of three places: the files, the garbage, or the shredder. Find

(or make) an attractive basket or file that matches your décor if you decide to keep it on your counter.

Hot Tips

- They say you should only touch paper once. I think those people are liars. That is hard to do. I have found the best way to handle papers the least amount of times is to try to deal with it at one sitting, when I have a few minutes.

- Take the pretty basket of papers and schedule time to go through it. Do you have a weekly television show you watch? That is the time to sort papers. Feel productive while you are watching that episode of "The Bachelor."

- Create a quick recycling center. Place a basket in a convenient section of your kitchen. Convenience is key. If you have to open a drawer or leave the room to recycle, chances are you won't. Yes, it takes up precious counter space, but you'll be living a bit "greener."

I've learned that organizing isn't about where we put things, it's about how we think about things, how we approach problems and healthier ways to do it.

~ Jean

Day 17

The drawer under the stove

Get people back into the kitchen and combat the trend
toward processed food and fast food.

~ Andrew Weil

Not every stove has a drawer at the bottom. Some manufacturers have started marketing a "warming drawer" on stoves. If you don't have a drawer, good news. You get to skip a day! But if you have a drawer, well, it's time to get down and dirty. Sorry.

If possible, remove the drawer completely and pull out the stove to clean the floor. Call in reinforcements; this can be a gross job. Wondering where that missing sock went? It could be under the stove. You may even find a pile of green fuzz. Here is a tip: Don't grab it with your bare hands; it could move and get you!

Pull everything out of the drawer and assess what you have.

Scrub the drawer. You might need a strong degreaser.

Figure out what you are actually storing in the drawer and see if it is under- or over-utilized. Maybe you discover the stove owner's manual and a broiler pan. For you, this is bonus storage space. Or perhaps your drawer is full of cookbooks you no longer use or frying pans with their lids. It really doesn't matter what you store here as long as it is a smart use of the space.

Remove anything you have not used in the last six to twelve months. Discard anything broken or damaged.

Assess what's left. This is one of those spaces where, whatever you do, the items need to be stored horizontally. You have two options: nest by putting the largest items on the bottom and working your way up to the smallest one or put the most-used items toward the top.

Hot Tips

- This drawer is an ideal space to store large items like long-handled grilling tools. Mine holds my big pizza pans and oversized cutting boards.
- Make sure that whatever you store is not heat sensitive. This drawer can get warm.
- Don't forget to scrub the sides of your oven. Food often drips into the little crack between your counter and stove. It's uncanny how objects and crumbs make their way down this tiny space.

I am thrilled with what I've accomplished this month in our kitchen. With your guidance, I've moved stuff around, discarded lots, and donated more. Thank you!

~ Wendy

Day 18

Cookie sheets and baking pans

Best way to get rid of kitchen odors: Eat out.

~ Phyllis Diller

I have been saying for years that horizontal is evil and that vertical is good. Simply put, the minute you start to pile things in a horizontal position, the ability to search becomes difficult.

Some kitchens are designed with cabinets that are specially made for cookie sheets and baking pans to be stored vertically in slots. However not all of us are so fortunate. We must think creatively.

Today is the day to assess the best use of your space.

Gather all of your cookie sheets and baking pans.

Wipe down the cabinet.

Take a serious look at the items you most often use. Can you store the ones that you rarely use in another area of the kitchen or house? Donate pans you don't use, or that you have not used in the last six to nine months.

Now look at the available space and the number of pans remaining.

Do you have the ability to store vertically? If so, locate a vertical organizer that meets your space needs. Don't limit yourself to the kitchen department. Some space organizers can be located in the office section of big box or office supply stores.

Do you need to adjust a shelf? Can you nest any of the pans together to take up less room? Cookie sheets and baking pans are best stored in a horizontal position, stacked and nested.

Hot Tips

- I find that many people have specialty baking pans for things like cheesecakes or Bundt cakes. They think they use these, but in reality they never do (unless of course they are bakers). Do you have pans that can be used multiple ways? If you own a cheesecake pan with a Bundt cake insert, dispose of your Bundt pan.

- How many items are you holding on to for sentimental reasons? Remember that gingerbread house mold I had for years and never used? I am giving you permission to donate those sentimental items you do not use or have room to store.

Okay, so this is a little nuts! I emptied my baking cupboard. I had eight cake pans stuffed in there along with seven cookie sheets. Kept only three of each. Feeling proud.

~ Jamie

Day 19

Pantry

The only thing that I have ever successfully made in the kitchen is a mess. And several little fires.

~ **Carrie Bradshaw,** "Sex In The City"

It is important to look at expiration dates as you go through your pantry. You will be shocked to discover some items expired two or three years ago. If you have food stored in other places besides your pantry, this is the time to sort it, as well. Gather boxes and cans to one place to see what you really have.

Start by pulling everything out.

Wipe down the shelves and drawers.

Discard anything old or stale products, foods you will never eat, or expired items. Unwanted foods nearing their expirations can be dropped off at a food pantry.

If food is in storage containers, take the time to empty the contents into temporary containers while you wash the originals. Make certain bins and jars are completely dry before you refill them.

Label each container.

Rearrange the shelves with the most-used items at eye level, less-used items placed higher or lower.

Create centers—areas where similar items are stored. This also produces an easy system when you need to make your grocery list. You can quickly scan your areas to see which foods are running low.

When I work with clients, I ask questions to find out how their household works. Every pantry tells a story. Lots of chocolate chips indicate a strong likelihood that someone in the family bakes. Would a baking center be desirable?

Sometimes I discover food for family members with health or dietary needs. What about a diabetic section with sugar-free snacks? A gluten-free area for someone with celiac disease? A basket of boxed mac and cheese for that picky toddler?

Here are some items commonly found in a pantry and how to organize them:

Spice packets/mixes: Think about storing all these together in a basket or storage container, so when you need one, you simply grab the whole basket to find it.

Canned goods: When you arrange cans and jars, picture in your mind how a grocery store aisle is organized. They don't have the soups with the chips and the spaghetti sauce with the peaches. Group fruits, vegetables, soups, beans, sauces. When you write out your grocery list, you'll know whether you need tomato soup.

Baking supplies: Dedicate a section of your pantry for anything baking related. Store cake mixes near chocolate chips, flour, and sugar if it's possible. When you crave snickerdoodles, you can gather everything from one location. Keep backup supplies separately. (If you do a lot of baking, you will often have extra bags of flour, sugar, and brown sugar. The extras take up room in the kitchen. Find space in a closet or cellar.)

Bags of chips: These can easily go stale after opening, so find a method that ensures freshness. Chips crush easily, so store them where they won't be smashed.

Paper products: Birthday napkins, paper plates and bowls, picnic supplies, paper towels, and plastic silverware deserve a place of their own. Decide how often these items are used and possibly keep them in another area of the house or garage.

You get extra credit for incorporating some of these bonus ideas:

Organize your pantry with ingredients for specific meals. For instance, assemble Mexican supper necessities (e.g. taco shells, seasoning, beans, rice, chips and salsa).

Place all varieties of pasta on one shelf. You might put it near tomato-based products often used with pasta. If you use anchovies when you make your grandmother's sauce, keep that here as well.

How about the jar of grated cheese? Or bottles of your favorite marinara sauce?

If you purchase specialty sauces and spreads, exotic nuts, cheese ball seasoning packets, and deli crackers for entertaining, keep them in a container. When unannounced company stops over, simply grab the bin and throw a party within a moment's notice.

Looking in my (newly organized) pantry, I see I am out of wild rice, graham cracker crumbs, and panko breadcrumbs. So the next time I need to make a recipe with any of those ingredients, I will know to buy them.

Hot Tips

- Shop more frequently. Now that I am an empty nester I shop daily like they do in Europe. My new kitchen is tiny and I do not have room for food storage. I find that I use all the ingredients when I shop daily, eliminating the need for a pantry.
- Place sticky bottles (think syrups and oils) on a turntable. Any spillover will be confined and easier to clean.

My pantry was a two-hour job. I cleared and wiped down all shelves, washed all storage containers, carried one of two stepstools to the lower level of my house, moved wayward spices to the spice cabinet, swept the floor, discarded unused small appliances—and found a beautiful glass salad bowl with a silver serving spoon/fork (which I polished ... with the tarnish solution I found a few days ago when I cleaned under my kitchen sink)! My kids say the pantry looks great and that I'm a good organizer. Ha!

~ Susan

Day 20

Fridge and fridge drawers

The kitchen really is the castle itself. This is where we spend our happiest moments and where we find the joy of being a family.

~ Maio Batali

Not only do we need to organize the inside of the refrigerator, but also what is on top of it—and possibly taped all over the front and sides. This large appliance quickly becomes a clutter magnet.

Take a hard look at what you have on display for everyone to see. What story does the outside of your fridge tell about you? Can you take some of the papers and place them in your information center? Do you really need the magnet from your insurance agent a decade ago? Could you place photos in an album or create a collage and place them in a frame?

If you must keep things on the fridge; try to group like items together. If you have more than one fridge, guess what ... you get to do this twice! Let's tackle the inside first.

Pull everything out.

Clean each shelf and drawer with warm, soapy water.

Keep only the things that you are going to use in the next couple of months. (I have some newly purchased salad dressing that tastes gross. Saving it is not going to make me use it. It is a reminder that I wasted money on it. I am going to throw it out!)

Check condiment expiration dates and keep only bottles that have not expired.

Group items as you return them to the fridge. Do you make sandwiches often? Put everything that you use to make sandwiches (meat, cheese, jelly, mayo, mustard, etc.) in a clear bin.

Place items you use most often at an easy-to-reach level. Dedicate a bottom shelf or drawer for juice boxes and other treats your small children expect.

Clean out any container that you are not keeping. Recycle glass and plastic as well as the metal lids.

Hot Tips

- Do not store anything in the door that needs to be kept very cold. I have found that milk does not keep as fresh there.

- Pull the refrigerator away from the wall and carefully clean its back and sides, as well as the wall and floor. What you find may shock you. Clean it up!

- What about those two inches between the fridge and the wall? If you are lucky enough to have a space like this, it is a perfect place for a broom and dustpan. Attach a small mop and broom organizer to the wall to keep them off the floor.

I have a cupboard above the fridge that is impossible to access so it will store my rarely used cake plate, Nordic ware, and good glasses. Everything else goes where I can reach and use it.

Thanks for the motivation!

~ Jean

Day 21

Freezer

Good food and a warm kitchen are what make a house a home.

~ Rachael Ray

D o you often throw things in the freezer and forget them? The Land of the Freezer-Burned Food is a long-lost relative of the vegetable crisper, aka The Vegetable Forgetter. This is a task that needs to be done quickly, so make sure you have fifteen minutes of uninterrupted time. If you have a deep freezer (chest or vertical) that you also use, it is your lucky day because you can add that in as well!

Pull everything out. Remember to be quick and/or recruit a helper in the interest of speed.

Wipe down the freezer. Warm soapy water may freeze. Hot gets the job done better as it won't have time to freeze before you wipe it down.

Use a large flat surface to help you sort quickly. Put all food into the trash that is beyond recognition or beyond anyone's desire to eat.

Divide food into groups: ice cream treats, meats, fruits, vegetables, leftovers. This method allows you to quickly search for supper items or to see what is on hand before you make a trip to the grocery store. Separate foods by shelves or purchase a few clear plastic bins.

Place older food toward the front to consume first. This works for food in all areas of your kitchen.

Keep frequently used items in the door of the freezer, where the temperature is not as consistent. Think frozen breakfast items that kids grab and use every morning.

Hot Tips

- I occasionally play Freezer Clean-out. The rules are simple: I try to avoid the store until everything in my freezer has been used. I make an exception if I have frozen sloppy joe meat but need buns (although chances are I have buns in the freezer as well). This game is good for your budget and your imagination; you get creative with those twelve bags of corn you bought on sale! Corn chowder, anyone?
- If you have more than one freezer, this is the day to tackle it. By going through all of this at once, you can take a good written inventory of what you currently have on hand. Store

the paper near the freezer and, as you use or add, keep your inventory updated.

🌳 If your deep freezer doesn't self-defrost, allow extra time for that chore.

A friend asked if there's a prize in this challenge. My response was that the good feeling of a job done well is reward in itself.

~ Susan

Day 22

Silverware drawer

If you look at the statistics, people spend
most of their time in the kitchen.

~ Vanilla Ice

This should be a short, quick day: one last drawer. I find that the typical silverware drawer holds so many more things than just spoons and forks. I find straws, baby spoons (the youngest child is seventeen), or plastic flatware from takeout restaurants.

You are a pro by now, right? But here's a reminder:

- Pull everything out.
- Wash silverware with warm, soapy water.
- Take a serious look at what you keep in this drawer. Try to focus just on the eating utensils. Do you have a matching or a mismatched set? I store my single set of

measuring cups and spoons in this drawer. (There is now room since I got rid of the baby spoons!)

- Sort out what should *not* go in this drawer. Where do those things belong?

- Get rid of anything you no longer use. Do you have serrated grapefruit spoons in the drawer, but you haven't bought a grapefruit in ten years? Goodbye grapefruit spoons!

- Now put everything back that belongs in the drawer.

Hot Tips

- Assess your silverware organizer. I like a mesh one where dust and crumbs can fall through, and I simply need to lift it to wipe out the drawer.

- I have two trays stacked on top of each other. On the bottom are the seldom-used utensils, like serving pieces and ladle.

- When I was kid we had a container on the kitchen table that held the silverware and napkins. It made setting the table much easier!

During pantry cleaning day, I found two boxes containing sixteen place settings of silverware purchased years ago when I was tired of my old, water-spotted silverware.

~ Susan

Follow-up thoughts

If I can teach you to organize your kitchen, I have taught you to organize your life.

~ MS Simplicity

I gave lots of advice about storing items you rarely use in another area of the home. I suggest that you put sticky notes on each item with that day's date on it. Set a goal: In six to twelve months from that date, you will donate those things you have not used. Be tough on yourself. It doesn't matter that Aunt Martha gave you the cow cookie jar. If you don't use it, get it out of your house. Let someone who loves cows or cookie jars become the new owner.

I want you to have a home filled with items you find beautiful and useful. That journey requires elimination of possessions you are keeping for all the wrong reasons. Most rational adults understand that you can't keep everything, even gifts they gave you.

So, how often should you go through this twenty-two-day process? I suggest at least once a year. The good news? If you were ruthless the first time, subsequent sweeps through your kitchen will be easy. I can now do some of my cabinets in only a few minutes.

To help keep things under control, simply set the kitchen timer at five minutes and find ten items you no longer use or need. Do this every few months and it will make the yearly process painless!

Checklist

- ☐ Day 1: Wipe the front of all cabinets
- ☐ Day 2: Cooking utensils
- ☐ Day 3: Plasticware
- ☐ Day 4: Specialty appliances and serving dishes
- ☐ Day 5: Pots and pans
- ☐ Day 6: Cookbooks and recipes
- ☐ Day 7: Family favorite recipes
- ☐ Day 8: Glasses and cups
- ☐ Day 9: Under the sink
- ☐ Day 10: Dishtowels, potholders, and trivets

☐ Day 11: Information center

☐ Day 12: **Junk drawers**

☐ Day 13: Plates and bowls

☐ Day 14: **Spices**

☐ Day 15: Food wraps and bags

☐ Day 16: **Kitchen counters**

☐ Day 17: The drawer under the stove

☐ Day 18: **Cookie sheets and baking pans**

☐ Day 19: Pantry

☐ Day 20: **Refrigerator and drawers**

☐ Day 21: Freezer

☐ Day 22: **Silverware drawer**

About the Author

Melissa Schmalenberger, aka MS. Simplicity, is an attorney-turned-productivity consultant who recently downsized her life and moved from Fargo, North Dakota to Bellevue, Washington. She works with clients via Skype, coaching calls, and in person. Melissa has been interviewed for *The Wall Street Journal, Costco Connection Magazine, Staples Online,* and *Organize 250+ Spring Cleaning Tips E-Zine.* A weekly columnist for *The Fargo Forum,* Melissa makes appearances as an organizing expert on multiple television and radio stations.

A vibrant mother, Melissa raised her three sons with her husband, Ray Ridl, at her side. Her imperfect life is often the place where she seeks inspiration as she simply strives to focus more time on the people she loves.

Connect with Melissa:

Facebook: https://www.facebook.com/melissaMSSimplicity

Blog: http://melissa-ididit.blogspot.com/

Twitter: @MS_Simplicty

Website: http://www.mssimplicity.com/

Instagram: https://instagram.com/ms_simplicity1/

YouTube: https://www.youtube.com/user/IDidItFargo

Pinterest: https://www.pinterest.com/mssimplicity/

Made in the USA
Lexington, KY
19 June 2018